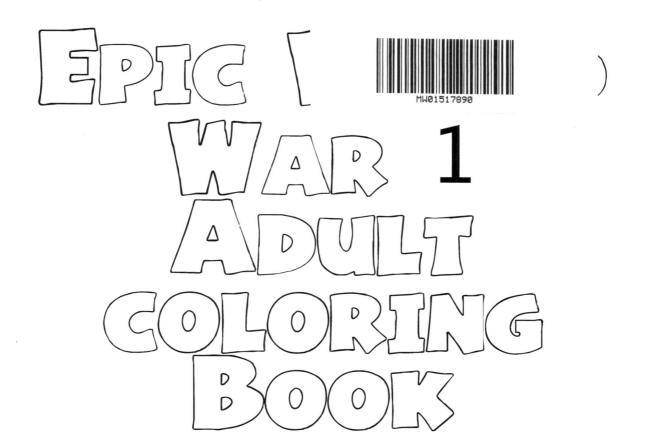

# Epic [ War 1 Adult Coloring Book

## BY SUSAN POTTERFIELDS

ISBN: 10: 1540607577
ISBN- 13: 978-1540607577

How would you like to be able to print off copies of your favorite coloring books?

How about having access to over a 1000's coloring books for the price of one coloring book every month.

Coupon Code to Join for only $1.00 for the first month when you sign up for the mailing list.

TRYTODAY

www.digitalcoloringbooks.com

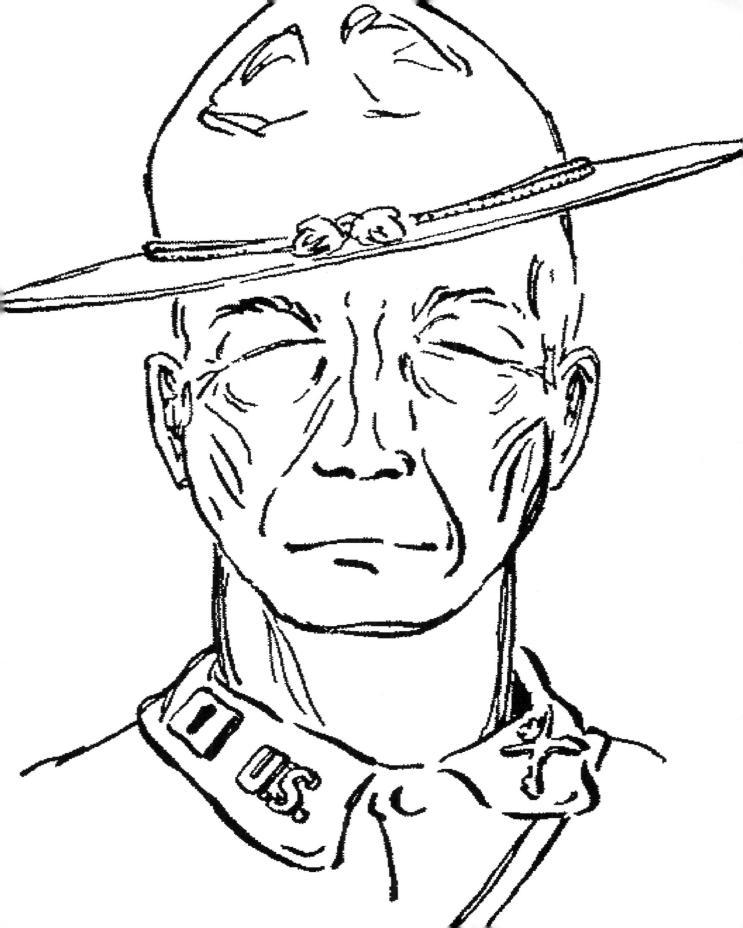

Susan Potterfields is a digital artist.  You can find more of her work on Amazon and digitalcoloringbooks.com.

38584395R00021

Made in the USA
Middletown, DE
22 December 2016